Stereograms of the Dead

Alistair Robinson

Red Squirrel Press

First published in 2008 by
Red Squirrel Press
PO BOX 219
MORPETH
NE61 9AU
www.redsquirrelpress.com

Cover design by Richard Fowler, Twentyseven Design
www.twentysevendesign.co.uk

Front flap drawing of R.Walker esq by Alistair Robinson

ISBN 978-0-9554027-8-4

Printed in England by Athenaeum Press Ltd.
Dukesway, Team Valley, Gateshead, Tyne & Wear
NE11 0PZ

Acknowledgements

Some of the poems in this collection have previously appeared in One2Five, South of Souter, Sand, Northern Lines and Moodswing and on Bee Postcards.

Contents

Wrestling With Kent Walton

If she were still a full ninety minutes,
my grandma would mourn the passing
of Billy Bremner and Emlyn Hughes.
She was a fan of the professional foul,
and the sort of sliding tackle that slid all the way
to the hoardings. She liked it best when the camera
got in tight and showed a twisted hairy leg.
It was then that Georgette Heyer would
lose her tussle with Georgie Graham.

My grandad, like most men once they've secured a wife,
wanted her to be someone else. He bought her
posh women's clothes and second-hand jewels
and when they went out he preferred it when she said
nothing. So she'd sit there and stare from the bus
window and be well behaved until
she saw someone slip on the pavement, or
lose their hat in the wind, and she'd
become the laughing policewoman and he'd blush.

When He stayed out alone on Saturday afternoons,
she'd rush back for wrestling with Kent Walton.
She loved a tight headlock and a mangled
encounter against the ropes, particularly if there'd have to be
a close-up of the forerunner of lycra with someone
big and sweaty in it. Then she'd imagine she too was
ringside, with all her uncouth unhusbanded sisters,
rooting for Giant Haystacks and spitting
obscenities and fragments of mints.

How she would have loved to have been a 3 a.m. girl,
to have come back tipsy with her high heels in her hand,
to have shopped at Ann Summers and sung karaoke,
and holidayed in Ayia Napa with her mates. She was made to
curse and flirt, not curtsey and kowtow.
She should have had her own credit card,
and a nippy little motor, and an account at the stand and tan.
All this and more … or maybe
not: she wouldn't have wanted to upset the old man.

Being Here

It's something unspoken, but we get close to it
when we speak of the weather, and the long line
of warm days, here where we wait for the mist.

With the old gardeners it has its romance tempered
with slang and sucked consonants.
With a few I could name it is sanctioned
with slaughter. Along the cliff we get nearer
to it still with an uneasy "mornin'" and a shared
scrutiny of the grass. It's something

to do with that pair of muddy bulls,
fighting in the field, who are even further
from acknowledging whatever it is,
and the lawnmower flutter of that fishing boat,
and the way the rock pools have been rolled out
like some new continent, and the soft
surprise of our breath. But we don't say it.

The World Of Mantovani

In the world of Mantovani,
Mantovani is no longer heard.
He's as silent as Jimmy Shand,
and the dog-eared John Denvers,
and all the Oklahoma!s
from the stereograms of the dead.

But still he smiles like he's
just back from the barber's
as he stares at incomplete jigsaws
and second-hand bras,
on unenchanted evenings
with Clive James's Brilliant Creatures,
by DM Thomas's White Hotel,
when the smell is not of saucisses St Germain,
but of something that the
dry cleaning failed to catch.

Morning

In the goals
the crossbar
bends under the
heavy quiet.
Black-headed gulls
in their away strip
pack midfield.

Nearby, a small lawn
stakes out its claim
to the light.

On the wasteland
two adventurers,
carrying a barrow
on a barrow, set off
to fetch the day.

A Mouth

In the picture I drew
of him four great-grand
children ago, my grandad
is frozen in patriarchal grand-

eur: mouth snatched in unequi-
vocal charcoal slash, staple-
edged, as it was etched
in life. No reminis-

cences splashed between
upper and lower stiff
lips: they allowed slight movement only for breath, ingest-

ion, pronouncements and
advice. But age has loosened
their lock as it has thawed
the glacier of his past.

Now he tells me of the
cupboard his father hewed
from the hillside beneath their house
and the shared shoes they

threw there to wear when
they were not chasing
hoops barefoot in the unmade
lane. The man who was

never known to acknowledge
the existence of defecation,
never mind partake in its
pleasures, relates the

arrival of the night-
soil men, scraping the middens
and loading the barges at
the end of the street where

London rocket sprouted in fertile
ballast hills. Now he curses
happily the slowing of his
mathematical response and shows

the gaps in his teeth
when he opens the midden
door to throw a bucket
of water at fleeing buttocks.

Birds (1)

Birds are always with us because

they can get away from us.

If the same could be said for zebra and gnu,

we'd see a lot of them too.

Outer Space Is Just Past Thirsk

Down here,
with our laws and privet hedges,
our insurance policies and tellies,
our museums and Marmite,
our histories of civilisation and our
lawn mowers, our philosophies and
our thermal underwear,
we're always,
and have always been,
just down from
up there.

Think of all the leagues of land
and ocean we crossed
to find the edge of our own backyard.
All that time the ends of the earth
were just above our heads.
Nowhere has always
been our nearest neighbour.
Think of all the spears and stones
we have thrown beneath its floor.

We're not talking light years.
Round here it goes like this:
Middlesbrough 24 miles,
Thirsk 50,
Outer space 62.

Outer space is just past Thirsk!

I'm going nowhere in a traffic jam
when the radio tells me how near it is.
Above, the route is clear.

Across the road
the giant rhubarbs
in the park
have taken on
a Venusian complexion.

Ghosts

I know this house by the speed of its
doors. I know air and I know gravity
and I know hinge grease. My children
watch the handles warily,
waiting for those who passed this way before
to pass this way again. But my
predecessors appear now only when I let them.
It is my ghost trails that throng the rooms.

This house has become mine beyond
the arrangement of cups. I am in the tick
of the clock and the smell of the drying clothes.
See the way that bowl rests on the drainer. See
the shadow the morning has lain on my floor.
But I will not haunt here. My children will take
the spirit of the place with them
and let me play in other halls.

The Old Town Hall, South Shields

It dates back to the days when
spacecraft were still made from

limestone. Ten sturdy legs, ideal for
touchdowns on deserts or

market squares, support a cockpit that doubles
as a council chamber. On the cobbles

one can see the scars of previous
take-offs; nearby are spent aluminium

cartridges that once held a sticky,
hops-based fuel. Entry is by steps

on the side of the fuselage; the stone
is worn by the many small steps of astronauts

and aldermen. The tip of the craft has been
tiled in slate and edged with lead

to provide protection against English rain
and the weather of any of the planets

on the Martian side of Earth.
At its apex is a devise for gripping

the surface of muddy or sandy worlds.
It can also be used as a weathervane.

The Invisible

Their flames lounge
in a driftwood hearth,
their smoke relaxes with the fog.

We have bought
VCRs, they say. We
have eaten from
Styrofoam. We have
tired of this chair,
gone for more of tins.

By chance they enchant
posterity. They let us
diagnose their dogs.

Birds (2)

They are like us, but also

completely different. They have

bits of bone-like stuff, sticking

off the front of their faces. Most

do colours better than us. We have been affronted

by their alternative mode of propulsion. They

don't need flutes. We will

catch them because they make it hard

for us to catch them. We will

eat them. We will display them. We will give them

meaning they do not need. When

we're Ancient Egyptian we will

wrap them in sack after they're dead and

fill their bodies with spices and give them faces like ours.

When we're clever we will laugh at such behaviour

and put all our impertinent observations in a book.

Kinship

I love those neglected bits of land
you sometimes find between buildings'
well-drawn lines, where the planner doodled
or spilt his coffee and now there is a stretch
of moss and maybe a broken bottle
or two and, when the sun goes down, rats.

And the roads, glimpsed from the train, that do nothing
except start and end where they do, on the edge
of a field, and which perhaps, one busy afternoon in
July, when the concrete was drying, seemed
to be heading somewhere, but became distracted.

Apart From The Odd Wild-Eyed Dog

Apart from the odd wild-eyed dog
one hears so little of the animal supernatural.
Rabbits rarely go a-haunting, it seems,
and likewise mole and geese and mackerel.
Unlike human slaughterhouses,
that have come to the end of their busy, spattered lives,
ex-abattoirs are suspiciously dull,
and seal-strewn coasts are bereft of ghosts
on the morning after the cull.

And for all their work within the frames of great artists
and the hours of fun they give,
heaven is, I understand, out of bounds (respectively)
to God's lambs and the family mastiff.
The Elysian Fields, we're told, are crowded with blokes
by the name of Ixion and Aenaeus and Lysander,
but in the parkland on high,
there's no bear, boar or fly,
or, come to think of it, antelope, yak or giant panda.

And yet the latest DNA research
says we're very nearly chimp:
only the width of a gnat's whiskers
separates us from *pan paniscus*..*
So is our extra 0.6 per cent
where we keep our souls and spirit stuff
or is all our talk of the afterlife
just self-deluding transparent guff?

* *the bonobo, or pygmy chimpanzee*

Polystyrene

A flock of polystyrene packing pieces
escapes from a builder's yard, surfs
the wind to beat the camber, arrives
gleefully where Villiers and Coronation streets meet.

Then the wind dies and the polystyrenes eye each other
apprehensively, huddle where the gravel chafes,
consider turning back but the wind catches
them again, and the boldest seize their chance.

How interesting the sofa shop car park seems
and the space beneath the cars, and the corner
where a flight of steps starts. Here they gather.
Some, stuck in a puddle of oil, are lost

to ambition when the wind returns, their idle
chatter echoing off the wall of another
yard, but the adventurers at liberty ride
the next gust. A straggler pauses, then follows.

Horizon

Where inland places
can pin their edges

to the map, and say
how far and where,

we look out to what?
A string across a vegetable plot.

And yet it confounds
the faulty theodolite of the mind.

Here ships at anchor pursue
the traveller on the shore.

Here clouds hide, but
we can not. Here footsteps

stop and flat worlds
bend. This is an island's

last field and that's
the world's end.

Sand Shoes

So many soles lost at sea.
Never uppers, just soles, mostly rubber
that fish and salt couldn't stomach, but
sometimes a flap of leather.

And so like fish,
as if pulled there by the current
of too strong a pun: boot fillets
with rusted nails as thin as kipper bones
and sliced plimsolls that must have danced
the seven seas since the heyday of Music and Movement.

Too many surely to have come downriver
with trees and shopping trolleys, they
tumble in with the tide, trying
to find their feet among fading footprints.

Unrequited Love

The field turns
fleet as the fell's

blood lusts for the
sea. Across the ruptured

map the car is
no longer a room

on wheels. Holst's
Rhapsody is drowned,

the contours smudge,
a forced ford

sets off the alarm.
It chimes with a siren

village: plates slotted
on drainers,

coats on pegs,
but only howling

dogs behind
flapping doors, down

river roads at
the valley's edge.

Arthur Street

"The fault line between a mythic past and 'real' past is not always easy to draw..."
Andreas Huyssen, 'Presents Past'

In my grandparents' house Borges lurked,
reading Conan Doyle in Braille.
The afternoons there were made for more than
northern present time:
Vermeer worked on biscuit lids
and did something to the clocks.
You could feel his oils in the light from the window.

The darkness we used looked like local stuff
and smelled of shoes, but if probed,
led to slower centuries still, where Bruegel's
huntsmen lurked and Richard Dadd's goblins.
If you listened carefully you'd hear
Jimmy Clitheroe above the screaming.

Then James Stewart would appear, in a '55 Rover,
and a barber who looked something like Peron.
And behind the last lane you crossed directly into Peru:
chickens scratched in the dirt,
and women in unravelling cardigans picked
potatoes. And where the wild birds flew
indoors a boy fell through the roof,
the moment Buddy Holly crashed.

Life's Little Indignities

How serene is the Buddha,

how imperturbable,

even when he's sitting in a barrow

with a label round his neck

in the forecourt

of a garden centre.

Unsundered Land
(a poem for Sunderland)

There is a sour pleasure
in riding the ring roads of the mind,
running in ever-decreasing circles
from the unknown outside,
knowing that every lane
that leads to the university
or the Stadium of Light,
returns eventually
to that martyred town hall site.

This is our offensive gyratory system,
carrying us, its sternest critics,
on our lamenting merry-go-round,
past roadworks that we alone
know will never end,
(scarring again this gum-stained hallowed ground)
on a one-way that a foreigner
could surely never fathom,
if a foreigner dared be found.

Nursing unhappy-hour pints
in sticky-carpet pubs,
we cross the bridge to count
ships we no longer build,
to watch coal being loaded
at a colliery long since closed.
We mourn the dearth of proper jobs,
the death of skills we knew as ours,
as we turn our faces against
the sharp North Sea and
the non-tidal treacherous hours.

Pointing a Daily Mail
at a lilac tower block,
we mutter this can not be right,
nor yet this shrine to glass.
St Peter's should be sanctified
by heaven-piercing cranes,
and our flagellated back-to-backs.
It's what Bede, our boy, would have wanted:
his centuries set in stone washed black.

Returning to our warming lager,
we drive with eyes half-closed.
Confident on our loop of tribal tarmac,
going wherever our tail lights go,
we conveniently bypass Tunstall Hill
and miss what we choose not to see:
a view over rooftops and centuries
and all this circuitous tired talk.
It's of a city ever-reborn, surprisingly green,
in a country unsundered by the A19.

School Photograph
(for Sheila Wakefield)

The photograph you show me is like a poem:
three lines of equal length, making a stanza as self-
contained as the school hall that surrounds it.
The bottom one has an obvious caesura in the full
stop of the teacher. The middle line I just don't
get; some of the phrases I can't put a name to,
but there are definite resonances. When I read those
expressions, I can see my own mistimed youth.

And like all good verse it lives with me after
the book is closed. The bit about you leads
me with you down the *cut* behind the *rec,*
as you figure out how far to go in the dark
and I'm thinking: nothing's changed – it's still
a winter's evening, and scary, after school.

The Lark Descending

It falls off its perch in the sky;

like a stunt pilot it tumbles

just to get us nervous –

a glissando down the neck of the violin,

then it pulls up just before

it smashes

into the grass.

Holy Trinity Church, Sunderland

Bill (gentle as a) Dove,
watches it from his tower block,
thus town hall and court room
and fire station of God,
whispers, despite his deafness,
when the wind gets up.

Full of prayer and Sunday dinner,
he rolls the cobbled carpet past the all-day boozer,
apologising for the compromise he's made
with nature and untidiness, letting
last week's leaves
keep out the draught.

Inside, it echoes to its non-existent congregation.
We see the churchwarden's seat
and the George the First font,
but God has quit them for
the cupboard in the vestry where
the packet of ginger biscuits waits,
and the litre of toilet cleaner,
and the brush and pan
Bill will use to sweep
the cobwebs from the altar.

Like A Man On A Wire

Above the scribbled thistles
a kestrel, as black as the folds
of the sea, as black as the morning
seagulls, balances on the air
like a man on a wire.

In My House By The Sea

Snails are racing
towards the Plimsoll

Line as the waters
rise. From my bed

I watch the kelp
dozing with the tide.

The ferry comes by
way of the roof

tops; Holland is
just over the lamp.

At night they light up
the edge of the

map just in case
we forget that it's

shaped like a dog on
its haunches. The

dove on the aer-
ial pilots us

'gainst the scudding clouds.
In the rook's bath

they keep a look-
out. Starlings feed on

the diced carrot of
legless passen-

gers. Many's the
night I've tended the

engine, jamming plas-
tic pegs and bi-

ros 'tween the cir-
cuit and the switch. Plumes

of steam signal to
the shore. At night-

break stowaway
bats take over from

the swifts trawling the
moths 'neath the storm

lantern. I'm No-
ah on Mount Ar-

arat with a
bath full of spiders.

Daddy Long Legs

The angels of late summer come nutting the telly,
confuse it and the ceiling for the sun.
Skating the air, they worship the fridge-glare like teenagers,
gift a leg when you demonstrate the difference
between double-glazed glass and outside.

Where In The World?

Resting binoculars on the dried-yolk
lichen of wall's mane, we stoop to see
a farther wall: a shoulder of hills and sloping
cliffs where England disappears into its map.

Then the same light that warms our fields and casts
whales on our waves, polishes a square of wheat
thirty miles south, and the Marske and Saltburn
churches and their bands of duny sand, and a TV mast
further still above Runswick Bay (or is it
Robin Hood's?), glisten in the hard night air.

When we drove there today we memorised landmarks
and angles of view, disappointed that northwards nothing
could be seen, but still we looked, forcing landscapes on the
glasses-field until a ship at anchor, close to our
house, danced in the morning mirage.

Looking south again, we put ourselves
in the picture, and the sun picks out only our windscreen
in the grey of Howdale Moor, or possibly Kettle Ness.

The Allotments of Eden

At dawn I hear the matins
bike, harmonising with

the gulls as the priest arrives, veiled
in half-mast saffron.

The ecumenical staircase
prayer mats are sodden,

the lino kneelers
treacherous, but the parishioners

wait, as they have all night,
pewed heads fixed on

incense rising
from eternal altar smoke

stacks. They don't flinch
when one of their number

is decapitated on the sacrificial
Formica worktop.

Now the priest is kneeling
on those forgotten

Islamic flourishes; he stares
at earth that cannot be

interpreted by the
uninitiated; he admires

his congregation – it is
odedient, cultivated. Outside

in the heathen fringe, fat
hen dances with abandoned gladioli.

The Afternoon After

(for Laura)

Our heads still full
of last night's quarrel
and lack of sleep,
we meet and have wheat
beer in a café that reminds us
of Paris: the rain, the paint
peeling artfully off the walls,
the stylishly naff
tariff board with the plastic
stick-on letters.

We pretend to be strangers,
try to look at each other
with unaccustomed eyes;
smile like we
didn't intend.

When I go to the bar
I feel my phone buzz in my pocket.
Your text says:
I love you.

The Shape Of The Week

For me it's like a line of ticker tape, folded:
short lengths for weekends,
long for weekdays,
and it doubles back on itself at the corner
of Monday morning.

And yet,
by Friday night
there are no parallel
lines.

And then it
folds again.

Flying To New York

Checking The Car

It is 3.30 a.m.
at the long-stay car park.

The man in the bus taxi
is watching me throw
a half-blue tangerine
across the tarmac.

On The Plane

The shutters are down
in this plastic afternoon.

I think we are inside
a hairdryer.

Deep Vein

At an altitude
slightly lower than
my complimentary ice cream
a thrombosis
is eyeing my deep veins.

Laura is dancing in her seat.

02/04

Scraping another sky
somewhere beneath this one
there are skyscrapers.
My plan is for us not
to scrape them.

The Raised Beach

This restharrow
will never snag

a plough, pushing
through pebbles that

the tide no longer
drags, with salted

bramble and lashless
oxeye, on a field

below the meadow
on a beach above

the shore, where grass
tangles with fishing

line and castles
are mainly soil.

This is where our
ancestors basked

when the ice
broke and the earth

moved, but rabbits
share our sea

air and spiders
cast the nets and

the waves are building
a new cliff where

land and sea
weeds meet.

On The Night Of The Eclipse

On the night of the eclipse
I fell asleep in front of an Ian Rankin thriller
and missed the twist,
then stood on a plug
as I searched for my shoes,
so was howling when
I finally faced the moon.

Then me and my missus fought
over the binoculars,
and I set off my Mp3 player
by mistake and as the light
turned orange we were
distracted by the oddity of sprouts
in next door's garden.

We looked back to see
the shadow of us
and everything else
racing across craters
towards the lunar north pole
and we were strangely silent.
Then I went to watch
Match Of The Day
and she read a book in bed.

Allotment George

Every morning, George, with his
1970s bank manager's glasses,
and his shiny shoes and regulation
boiler suits he wears like pin-stripe,
turns up with the newspaper under his arm,
as if arriving at the City. He takes no
obvious pleasure from this activity:
this is work, he gets no breaks –
Christmas Day and bank holidays he is here.
Doing whatever it is he does.

Apart from his paper, he takes
very little down the garden path
but brings much back. When
the council sends the skip he produces,
as if from a magician's hat,
all manner of scrap.

Now George is retiring from his
unforgiving recreation
I imagine him swapping it for
a leisurely occupation,
see him whiling away his twilight years
in an office.

Fairweather Friends

The flowers we planted,
the cabbages we fed,
the trees we sat under
are on their own tonight.

The privet and buddleia
that sheltered us from the
sea breeze of summer
have only themselves to save.

Shackled by the roots,
they attempt to flee.
Feet away, behind the wall,
horses queue for calm.

Sunday Observance
(On Seeing Stella McCartney's Crystal Horse at Belsay)

He stood on the edge
like Eugene Levy with an umbrella.
Sunday had dragged him here,
and had splashed his good beige slacks.
It had said: come and see this place,
forsake all others, see only
this crystal horse between these castle walls.

Avuncular disdain
was his special gift. He lavished it now,
as motions were gone through
and about a mile of dolomite mud.
How much better to be those boys he saw
spurning the exhibitions to poke beneath
the castle hearth for something living.

And so he and his wife
and her friend and her husband
returned, frittering their precious third age, he felt,
as she and her friend talked
and he and his did not,
until fate framed two bullfinches
in an old quarry hollow
and he recognised something quite subversive.

After The Storm

The burn is contrite
now, stays in its bed

when the rain returns.
It has combed the hair

of the bank it ravaged,
left shame-faced

snowdrops there,
and where the turf

was flayed and scored
offers boiled fluorspar

sweets. Sometimes the rocks
must be caged

to be saved. Here, a limestone, alluringly lichen-

tattooed, turns into
a waking frog.

Tongue/Spit

Beneath the sea fret
redshank shelter,

a jogger exists only
in his cough;

sprigs of gull
are pressed to the beach

like curls
on a sweating brow.

Is this a tongue of water
or a spit of sand?

The Bodgers*

People paid us to stay out of their fragile houses,
that's how we made our money. We used it to buy
a beech coppice, a long way off. We shared the driving;
it was uneventful. There were long silences, interspersed
with football talk. Sometimes we'd start off in third and stop
at green lights, but our accidents were mostly minor, caused
by staring at cows and clouds at right angles to the road.

The trouble started with the shelter. We had the instructions, they were
incomplete. We swore at them and at each other. By nightfall
we had only one wall up. We slept in the car. It was a misty
night. Next day we were keen to get at our coppice.
We got out our tools: the bread knife, the pack of screwdrivers from
Everything's A Pound, an axe we'd use to open
a paint tin, and a brace of model-maker's hacksaws.

After an hour I was hanging off branches; he was hurling rocks which the
coppice hurled back. We shouted at the wood and each other.
We broke the hacksaws in hacking. There was blood on the cheese when we
broke for lunch. There was blood on the bread knife
when we used it to shave a tree to chair-spindle thickness.

By sundown we had enough for a three-legged footstool,
and two of those had been Sellotaped, badly.
Meanwhile the shelter was still mostly flat-packed on the grass.
It was then that the man from the Bodgers' Guild
came round and rescinded our membership.

**As a bodger (or botcher) of many years' standing, I was intrigued to discover there used to be another kind of bodger: a tinker who would buy a coppice, build a shelter at the site, and lathe the wood to make spindles for chair legs. I imagined myself and my late father, also an inveterate bodger, bodging bodging.*

Domestic Science

The surface of the gravy is rippling,

as if something below is breathing,

and the dimpled dusky skin

is just the parchment of a cocoon.

But it's not some beefy Bisto beastie

that is lurking with the dumplings,

but the obedient fidgeting molecules

of microwaved lumpy granules.

Marmalade And Carbon Monoxide

Oranges were not only the only scent that day –
there was the dog, back from the rain.
The master had a similarly discerning snout.
All the elbowing, blokish smells from the lab
could have popped round for a smoke,
and he would have picked each one out.
And he wouldn't have been embarrassed by
this gentle, girlish chemistry on this
domestic Bunsen burner.

The dog, he was busy with his rabbits and his dung –
he could juggle them with the mandarins.

Of all the people it might have tricked,
the stealthy gas went for them,
entirely fairly but it seemed like arrogance:
the chemist and his spaniel.

Beyond The Dewey Decimal System

There's a place for everything at the library.
All subjects are properly
housed, even those
that don't have a place in the
Dewey Decimal System.

For instance, beneath the opening hours,
above the city crest,
there's a shelf
for mangy pigeons.

A Letter To Our Unborn Child

You don't know us
but soon we'll be very close …
and then distant, probably,
and then close again, I hope.

You seem surprisingly clever.
While your mam was getting
stressed about work and I was
taking the dog for a walk you were
busy forming fingers and lungs
and doing some really complicated
stuff which we wouldn't
have a clue about.

We hope you bring your cleverness –
and your precocious dexterity – with you.
And when you get here
I'll help you with your cleverness,
if that's OK, and I promise
to follow Government guidelines
and spend the right amount of time
doing homework with you,
and not for you.

You need food for brains –
we've seen the menu in the
pregnancy book. We'll read it
out to you if you like.
If there's anything you particularly
require, just kick. The book
says you can start doing that from
next Tuesday week. But then,
you probably knew that.

Waiting

We sit on the bachelor settee
and wait.
The stereo is playing a song
that I loved the year you were born.
You crunch ice,
your only craving;
I slip my hand in your hand,
we admire the handles
of our new kitchen units.

Most of the stuff
has been done now.
Outside the swallows have returned,
the spiders are awake,
the boy racers are duelling
in the spring car park.
Across the river
Admiral Collingwood stands,
ships come and go,
the daughter of my first marriage
looks for her shoes, waits
a while in the porch, then
leaves.

Your mother says its head is now

The size of the plaster Buddha

on the sideboard.

In the waiting rooms

we wait.

Two Alaskan Poems

(i)

The Bachelors of Ketchikan Creek

Below the bordello boardwalk,
sockeye salmon slug it out
like prospectors after the gold rush.

Mad as fuck, and knackered,
they ignore the ravens
and the gawping tourists,

slap tattooed muscle
on the slab of water.

(ii)

The Bear Who Wasn't There

You were scarier than
the bears we did see –

you were a ghost
but your *scat* was hot.

It looked like
wholemeal berry muffins.

We could smell the hole
you'd made through the forest;

you smelled bad
for a ghost.

The river here was your barrel:
you put your paws in

and took the tired brains
out of salmon,

let them rest at last.

Quark The Dog

I'm thinking of writing to Stephen Hawking
about our dog. I left a book about quantum physics
by her basket and I think she's got the hang of it.
I'm going to call her "quark".

She's on her way to perfecting
the art of leaving a point in space just as
she is arriving at it. That point is usually
marked by a stick, or a length of oarweed.
Once she experimented with an old Newcastle United
scarf that had been half buried in sand
blown from the beach.

Not all her experiments are successful.
I understand that much of the great
scientific work is like this. Sometimes
she can carry off the stick just
as she is picking it up.
Sometimes she carries it off
without picking it up.

Mites

In the carpet shop there's a photograph
of a muscular animal that stalks the shag pile
and has colonised my bed. They say
you are never more than 20 feet from a rat,
but this little bastard is closer still.

The salesman says the carpet we're on now
has not been protected in the way
that my new berber will be
when I fork out the extra £100
for something better than Scotch Guard.

He's shaken a bed and magnified them.
They're not content to wait for me to shed my skin –
they're prepared to come and get it.
They're making the ascent to my pants as we speak.

Back home I take an axe to my king-size,
just in case they're in the wood,
and out it goes with the bug metropolis that is my mattress,
and the teaming planes that were
my Axminster and the underlay.

It is hopeless, I know.

I stalk the boards
some time after midnight
and listen to the traffic.

The Fridge, the Salsa Dip and the Individual Caramel Dessert

At the back of my fridge
there is a Narnian arrangement of physics:
people reach in from another dimension
and leave half-full jars of salsa dip
and individual caramel desserts
and then forget about them
and expect me to clear them out.

Cormorants

(i)

Barely troubling the air,
they stay as close to the water

as a skimming stone,
racing their shadows

from Marsden Bay
to Coxgreen Bridge, inscrutable,

unswervable, staying solitary,
even in threes.

(ii)

On the weir,
they wait for the river

to bring their meals to them;
feigning boredom

they hang their wings
out to dry,

appear distracted
by the traffic

over the bridge,
look almost bothered

by the black-headed gulls
next in line.

Manifesto

We should all go out
in small boats to greet our

neighbour, the sea. We
should cast flowers

upon the water, and turn
to the shore as ships and waves

have done, and point out
steeples and chimneys and

the illuminated advertisements
of garage forecourts. Back

on land cursory glances from
the upper decks of buses will

be banned. We should be made
to spend whole days staring

towards Denmark and the coast
of Schleswig Holstein, imagining

another people, surprisingly similar
speaking a related tongue, equally

unaware of a lost kinship, equally,
shamefully blase about their oceanic

nature. We should rejoice when
our sea invades our air, when she

caresses us when we're sunbathing,
or belches her fishy lunch, or hangs

about on November Tuesdays like a lank
and sullen teenager. We should bring

tourists to see our corroded cars and
flaking window frames. We should

hail the fisherman and the weekend sailor. We
should make the lobster pot our symbol.

We should have parties to marvel at the
moon glade and sunrise and the curvature

of the earth. We should commit the tides
to memory and weave our day with their ebb

and flow. But let's start with that boat
trip and a bouquet to throw.

If I Were A God

If I were a god,
I'd lay my cheek
against the Amazon rainforest
and let the parrots fly
in my hair.

If I were a god,
I'd run my tongue
along the Western Isles
and let the salmon splash
in my mouth.

If I were a god,
I'd cup the Wear Rail Bridge
in my hands
and blow it
like a harmonica.

If I were a god,
I'd put my lips
to every ear
and whisper:
"It'll be all right."

The Day The Swallows Weren't There

From the steaming trees they rose:
giddy with number,
the flies fucked
and did threesomes
on the hot cars.

Sunlight On Pavement

At about the time my grandmother would have put on her lipstick
and taken me on the bus to the big town, I take her
hand. The sun has just emerged from a cloud and it's
belting off pavements and back gardens, reminding me,
as it always does, of how we used to be:
walking down the lane to the bus stop, us full of dinner,
her smelling of lipstick, and me wondering if my grandma
was old and beginning to panic in case she was.

The sun is warming the patios across the street
from the home and it's reminding me more of her
than she does herself. I look into her face
and see only other old women.

Suddenly the real Eileen comes out,
I've talked to her and been explained to her and
nothing happens, and then, with her hand in mine,
her face changes, and her hair seems to, and her head
comes out of its slump.

                                        Sometimes she sees the real
me, and she remembers those bus rides, in the single-decker –
climbing the hill by the egg farm and the field with the scraggy
ponies, with the afternoon sun catching the wickens grass
and making it hurt to look out of the window,
and us shielding our eyes to see the verge
where a photo was taken, with her in a sheepskin coat,
and me and my brother, in hand-knitted sweaters,
being led by the hand. And I remember the rituals we enacted
on my behalf, the games which had her humouring me.

At other times I am just a younger bloke,

and she flirts a bit and strokes my uncallused hands
and says I've never done a hard day's work.

Today, the sun stays out but she dies down.
"I'm leaving," she says. "I'm sick of being here,
and I'm sick of being told what to do by you."

In pictures around the wall the real Eileen
is large and smiling. She is always with children; now
she is a child once more and we return to childhood with her.
We get her to name the occupants of the street where she was born.
She dredges up sisters Claire and Ena, and the father
of Jimmy Mitchell, the writer. But now she is childless.
My mother and me we're just adults who flit in and out of
anonymity.

Later on the rhymes she used to sing to us are sung to her.
We don't say anything; we're none of us young.

At last the whole big event takes its toll on my grandfather,
famed for his stoicism, celebrated for his spurning of religion.
At first he slags off the weathermen, the nurses, the matron.
And then, as we're creeping out and can hear her upstairs,
he says to me: "What a life."

And when we try to talk
about football nothing comes. I put on my sunglasses.

In The Shadow Of The Volcano

In the shadow of the volcano
lie the hounds of Pompeii.
Quiet as mosaics,
stuck with chewing gum and cigarette ends,
they mock the descendants of those who said:
beware of the dog.

Zen And The Art Of The Tea Ceremony

In his timber yard
sparrows play,
rain falls.
By his wheel,
cherry wood dries.

Already it has begun.

A gentlewoman enters.
In the boot of her hatchback
there are bottles for the bottle bank,
and broken dolls.

The potter does conjuring tricks
for her daughters: what is the sound
of an empty paper bag?

He tells them how his bellows
once fed pellets to
the Duke's pheasants.

Now they feed his fire.
Cherry smoke fills the street.

He takes rain from his roof,
dirt from the hills,
loads his brush with ash and rust.

They watch. At last:
a cup for the finest
leaves, the brightest water.

He places it on a shelf,
and sips day-old tea
from a chipped mug.

Spam

Truman Streitmatter, Krystyna Culp,
Expectant H Accreditation,
Concepcion Pilkington, Efren
Waller, Ruggedness G Epistem-

ology, Lillie V Singleton,
Jerri Miranda, Edelmira
Lamey, Elbe Schafer, Kent Oli-
varez, Caitlin Valencia, Heath

T Shelton, Sumatra Rains, Luther
Grayson, Maximo Eddings, Urin-
ary B Banalest, Augustine
N Jarrett, Eloy G Swift, Dante

Juarez, Wade McGuinness, Ali F
Delarosa, Crossarm Hale, Dwight Venk-
ler, Avalanche Rosario, Spec-
trum H Reinvented, Octavi-

o G Kelley, Indigo Lundahl,
Jeremiah Lawless, Bleak Batemen,
Gonzales Driscoll, Dumbell Hoover,
Cialis, Valium, Viagra.